Knowing Jesus Christ

BOOK ONE OF THE STUDIES IN CHRISTIAN LIVING

*A NavPress resource published in alliance
with Tyndale House Publishers, Inc.*

NAVPRESS○

NavPress is the publishing ministry of The Navigators, an international Christian organization and leader in personal spiritual development. NavPress is committed to helping people grow spiritually and enjoy lives of meaning and hope through personal and group resources that are biblically rooted, culturally relevant, and highly practical.

For more information, visit www.NavPress.com.

Knowing Jesus Christ

Copyright © 1964 by The Navigators. All rights reserved.
Revised edition copyright © 1981 by The Navigators. All rights reserved.

A NavPress resource published in alliance with Tyndale House Publishers, Inc.

NAVPRESS and the NAVPRESS logo are registered trademarks of NavPress, The Navigators, Colorado Springs, CO. *TYNDALE* is a registered trademark of Tyndale House Publishers, Inc. Absence of ® in connection with marks of NavPress or other parties does not indicate an absence of registration of those marks.

Scripture taken from the Holy Bible, *New International Version*,® *NIV*.® Copyright © 1973, 1978 by Biblica, Inc.® Used by permission. All rights reserved worldwide.

For information about special discounts for bulk purchases, please contact Tyndale House Publishers at csresponse@tyndale.com or call 800-323-9400.

ISBN 978-0-89109-077-9

Printed in the United States of America

28 27 26 25 24 23 22
44 43 42 41 40 39 38

Not by Bread Alone

"Man does not live on bread alone, but on every word that comes from the mouth of God."*

Nearly two thousand years ago, Jesus Christ repeated those words which had been spoken by Moses many centuries earlier. Just as in Moses' time and in Jesus' time, those words are still true today.

People everywhere are turning to a serious study of the Bible as they recognize the hunger in their heart that only God's words can satisfy. Both new Christians and those who have known Christ for many years need to study the Bible for their spiritual health and growth.

Studies in Christian Living is designed to help you . . .
> establish a program of personal Bible study.
> learn and practice the essentials of a well-rounded Christian life.
> develop skills allowing you to continue Bible study on your own after completing this series.

It is important to work through each book in Studies in Christian Living in order. The books build progressively, so you won't want to skip any of them.

You need only a Bible to begin. Each question will direct you to a passage of Scripture. Look up the passage, think about it, and write the answer in your own words.

References to passages in Scripture are given in this

---

*Deuteronomy 8:3 and Matthew 4:4.

way; Revelation 3:20. This means the book of Revelation, chapter three, verse twenty.

Try to work on these studies frequently. By answering only three or four questions a day, you can finish a chapter each week.

Be sure to ask God in prayer to give you understanding as you study.

The chapter topics in this book are:
- Who Is Jesus Christ?
- The Work of Jesus Christ
- Eternal Life in Christ

CHAPTER ONE

Who Is Jesus Christ?

Jesus once asked his followers, "Who do people say I am?"
They replied with a few of the opinions the public had of him at that time. Then Jesus said, "But what about you? Who do you say I am?" (Matthew 16:15).
That question was important then—and it's just as important today. The answer is the foundation for true life.

Jesus Christ Is God

1. The Old Testament prophet Isaiah foretold much about a future great servant of God, and his words were fulfilled hundreds of years later by Jesus Christ. What did Isaiah say in Isaiah 9:6 about the titles Christ would have?

   _____
   _____
   _____
   _____

2. How did Peter answer Jesus' question in Matthew 16:15-16?

   _____
   _____

3. Read the account of Jesus walking on the water in Matthew 14:22-33. After his disciples saw this, what did they do? (verse 33)

_____

_____

4. What did Jesus claim about himself in Matthew 28:18?

_____

_____

5. How did Jesus demonstrate his power in Mark 1:40-42?

_____

_____

6. What power does Jesus claim to have in John 5:21?

_____

According to what Jesus said in John 5:40, why do some people not experience what Jesus has to offer?

_____

7. In John 5:22-23, what attitude toward the Son of God did Jesus teach that we should have?

_____

8. Read in John 10:22-33 about a dramatic confrontation Jesus had with some Jews. How did Jesus identify himself with God the Father? (verse 30)

_____

Why did the Jews who heard him speak these words prepare to stone Jesus? (verse 33)

_____

9. Read in John 20:24-28 about the doubts the disciple Thomas had about Jesus Christ's resurrection. What did Thomas say when Jesus later appeared to him? (verse 28)

_____

10. Are you convinced Jesus Christ is God? If so, why?

___

Jesus Christ's Humanity

11. How is Jesus shown to be human in these verses?

    John 4:6 ___

    John 11:35 ___

    John 19:28 ___

12. According to Hebrews 2:14, why did Jesus come to earth to live as a human being and to die?

___

13. Read Hebrews 4:14-15. According to verse 15, how was Jesus like all other people?

___

    How was he different?

___

CHAPTER TWO

The Work of Jesus Christ

Jesus healed the sick, raised the dead, fed hungry multitudes, and was a friend to social outcasts and sinners. He spoke words of wisdom and power which astounded his hearers. He lived a sinless life, but was put to death as a common criminal.

But his story doesn't end there. His death, his resurrection, and his ascension into heaven mark the most amazing aspects of his life on earth.

His Death

1. When the angel told Joseph about the coming birth of Jesus (Matthew 1:21), for what purpose did he say Jesus was coming into the world?

   _____

   _____

2. Read Matthew 16:21. To whom did Jesus talk about his coming suffering, death, and resurrection?

   _____

3. According to Matthew 27:26, what kind of death did the Roman governor Pilate sentence Jesus to?

   _____

4. What kind of men were executed with Jesus? (Matthew 27:38)

   _____

5. According to Romans 5:8, what did the death of Jesus prove about God?

   _____

6. Read carefully the prophecy in Isaiah 53:5-6. Why did Jesus Christ suffer?

   _____

   How is man's sinful attitude described?

   _____

   _____

   Who put the punishment for our sin on Christ?

   _____

7. Read 1 Peter 2:24. For what purpose did Christ bear our sins?

   _____

   _____

8. Read Jesus' words in John 10:17-18. Check one of the following statements which is the best summary of these verses:

   ☐ Jesus went to his death voluntarily, and God loved him for this.
   ☐ Jesus was forced to a premature death by the actions of his enemies.
   ☐ Jesus did not resist his suffering and death because he knew he was powerless to avoid it.

His Resurrection

9. Read John 2:18-22. What did Jesus say would happen to him after he was killed?

   _____

10. In Peter's speech near the temple recorded in Acts 3, what did he proclaim in verse 15?

    _____

    _____

11. According to Acts 4:33, in what manner did the apostles talk about the resurrection of Jesus Christ?

    _____

12. Read Romans 1:4. What did the resurrection demonstrate about Christ?

    _____

13. According to Paul's words in 1 Corinthians 15:3-8, what people saw Jesus Christ after his resurrection?

    _____

    _____

    _____

    _____

14. According to 1 Corinthians 15:17, why is Christ's resurrection so important for each of us?

    _____

    _____

His Ascension

15. Read Acts 1:9-11. Where did Jesus ascend to?

    _____

16. In John 14:1-2, for what reason did Jesus tell his disciples he was going to heaven?

    _____

17. In John 14:3, what else did he promise?

    _____

    _____

18. Read Paul's statement of prayer in Ephesians 1:18-23. Over how much does Christ now rule? (verses 21-22)

   _____
   _____

19. Review the questions and your answers in this chapter. Have you learned something that is especially important to you? If so, write it down here, and explain how it can help you:

   _____
   _____
   _____
   _____
   _____
   _____

CHAPTER THREE

Eternal Life in Christ

In every age of history men seek to know the secret of life after death. All of us have only a short period of time on earth, and then we must face eternity.

What does it mean to have eternal life, and how do we get it? The Bible gives us the answers.

The Source of Eternal Life

1. Read John 3:36. What people have eternal life?

   _____

   What happens to everyone else?

   _____

   _____

2. In John 14:6, what did Jesus claim about the way in which people can reach God?

   _____

   _____

3. How did Jesus define eternal life in John 17:3?

   _____

   _____

4. In Peter's speech in Acts 4:10-12, what did he say about the source of salvation?

   _____

   _____

5. What condition affecting all mankind is stated in Romans 3:23?

   _____

6. Read Romans 6:23. What results from sin?

   _____

   Where does eternal life come from?

   _____

How Do We Receive Eternal Life?

7. According to John 1:12, what response to Christ must we have in order to become God's children?

   _____

8. Read John 11:25. What does Jesus promise?

   _____

   _____

9. In Acts 10:43, what did the prophets say we receive when we believe in Christ?

   _____

10. Read carefully 1 John 5:11-12. If someone has Christ, what else does he have?

    _____

    Can he have this without having Christ?

    _____

11. According to Ephesians 2:8-9, do our own accomplishments which we achieve in life have anything to do with our being saved? Why or why not?

Can We Know We Have Eternal Life?

12. When Jesus promised eternal life to those who hear and believe him in John 5:24, with what phrase did he begin his promise?

13. According to Romans 8:35-39, what can cut us off from Christ's love?

14. Read 2 Thessalonians 3:3. What will God do for us?

15. Read 1 John 5:13. What is it that we can <u>know</u>?

A Summary Verse

16. Read John 3:16. Who did God love?

    What did God's love cause him to do?

    What happens to those who believe in his Son?

17. Do you know that you have eternal life?

Why or why not?

_____
_____
_____
_____

Scripture Passages

Chapter One: Who Is Jesus Christ?

Isaiah 9:6	For to us a child is born, to us a son is given, and the government will be on his shoulders. And he will be called Wonderful Counselor, Mighty God, Everlasting Father, Prince of Peace.
Matthew 16:15-16	"But what about you?" he asked. "Who do you say I am?" [16]Simon Peter answered, "You are the Christ, the Son of the living God."
Matthew 14:22-33	Immediately Jesus made the disciples get into the boat and go on ahead of him to the other side, while he dismissed the crowd. [23]After he had dismissed them, he went up into the hills by himself to pray. When evening came, he was there alone, [24]but the boat was already a considerable distance

The passages on this and the following pages are from The New International Version of the Bible, © 1978 by the International Bible Society.

from land, buffeted by the waves because the wind was against it.

²⁵During the fourth watch of the night Jesus went out to them, walking on the lake. ²⁶When the disciples saw him walking on the lake, they were terrified. "It's a ghost," they said, and cried out in fear.

²⁷But Jesus immediately said to them: "Take courage! It is I. Don't be afraid."

²⁸"Lord, if it's you," Peter replied, "tell me to come to you on the water."

²⁹"Come," he said.

Then Peter got down out of the boat and walked on the water to Jesus. ³⁰But when he saw the wind, he was afraid and, beginning to sink, cried out, "Lord, save me!"

³¹Immediately Jesus reached out his hand and caught him. "You of little faith," he said, "why did you doubt?"

³²And when they climbed into the boat, the wind died down. ³³Then those who were in the boat worshiped him, saying, "Truly you are the Son of God."

Matthew 28:18

Then Jesus came to them and said, "All authority in heaven and on earth has been given to me."

Mark 1:40-42

A man with leprosy came to him and begged him on his knees, "If you are willing, you can make me clean."

⁴¹Filled with compassion, Jesus reached out his hand and touched the man. "I am willing," he said. "Be clean!" ⁴²Immediately the leprosy left him and he was cured.

John 5:21

"For just as the Father raises the

	dead and gives them life, even so the Son gives life to whom he is pleased to give it."
John 5:40	"You refuse to come to me to have life."
John 5:22-23	"Moreover, the Father judges no one, but has entrusted all judgment to the Son, 23that all may honor the Son just as they honor the Father. He who does not honor the Son does not honor the Father, who sent him."
John 10:22-33	Then came the Feast of Dedication at Jerusalem. It was winter, 23and Jesus was in the temple area walking in Solomon's Colonnade. 24The Jews gathered around him saying, "How long will you keep us in suspense? If you are the Christ, tell us plainly."

²⁵Jesus answered, "I did tell you, but you do not believe. The miracles I do in my Father's name speak for me, ²⁶but you do not believe because you are not my sheep. ²⁷My sheep listen to my voice; I know them, and they follow me. ²⁸I give them eternal life, and they shall never perish; no one can snatch them out of my hand. ²⁹My Father, who has given them to me, is greater than all; no one can snatch them out of my Father's hand. ³⁰I and the Father are one."

³¹Again the Jews picked up stones to stone him, ³²but Jesus said to them, "I have shown you many great miracles from the Father. For which of these do you stone me?"

³³"We are not stoning you for any of these," replied the Jews, "but for blasphemy, because you, a mere man, claim to be God."

John 20:24-28	Now Thomas (called Didymus), one of the Twelve, was not with the disciples when Jesus came. [25]When the other disciples told him that they had seen the Lord, he declared, "Unless I see the nail marks in his hands and put my finger where the nails were, and put my hand into his side, I will not believe it." [26]A week later his disciples were in the house again, and Thomas was with them. Though the doors were locked, Jesus came and stood among them and said, "Peace be with you!" [27]Then he said to Thomas, "Put your finger here; see my hands. Reach out your hand and put it into my side. Stop doubting and believe." [28]Thomas said to him, "My Lord and my God!"
John 4:6	Jacob's well was there, and Jesus, tired as he was from the journey, sat down by the well. It was about the sixth hour.
John 11:35	Jesus wept.
John 19:28	Later, knowing that all was now completed, and so that the Scripture would be fulfilled, Jesus said, "I am thirsty."
Hebrews 2:14	Since the children have flesh and blood, he too shared in their humanity so that by his death he might destroy him who holds the power of death—that is, the devil.
Hebrews 4:14-15	Therefore, since we have a great high priest who has gone through the heavens, Jesus the Son of God, let us hold firmly to the faith we profess. [15]For we do not have a high priest who is unable to sympathize

with our weaknesses, but we have one who has been tempted in every way, just as we are—yet was without sin.

Chapter Two: The Work of Jesus Christ

Matthew 1:21   "She will give birth to a son, and you are to give him the name Jesus, because he will save his people from their sins."

Matthew 16:21   From that time on Jesus began to explain to his disciples that he must go to Jerusalem and suffer many things at the hands of the elders, chief priests and teachers of the law, and that he must be killed and on the third day be raised to life.

Matthew 27:26   Then he released Barabbas to them. But he had Jesus flogged, and handed him over to be crucified.

Matthew 27:38   Two robbers were crucified with him, one on his right and one on his left.

Romans 5:8   But God demonstrates his own love for us in this: While we were still sinners, Christ died for us.

Isaiah 53:5-6   But he was pierced for our transgressions,
    he was crushed for our iniquities;
the punishment that brought us

> peace was upon him,
> and by his wounds we are
> healed.
> ⁶We all, like sheep, have gone
> astray,
> each of us has turned
> to his own way;
> and the Lord has laid on him
> the iniquity of us all.

1 Peter 2:24 — He himself bore our sins in his body on the tree, so that we might die to sins and live for righteousness; by his wounds you have been healed.

John 10:17-18 — "The reason my Father loves me is that I lay down my life—only to take it up again. ¹⁸No one takes it from me, but I lay it down of my own accord. I have authority to lay it down and authority to take it up again. This command I received from my Father."

John 2:18-22 — Then the Jews demanded of him, "What miraculous sign can you show us to prove your authority to do all this?" ¹⁹Jesus answered them, "Destroy this temple, and I will raise it again in three days."

²⁰The Jews replied, "It has taken forty-six years to build this temple, and you are going to raise it in three days?" ²¹But the temple he had spoken of was his body. ²²After he was raised from the dead, his disciples recalled what he has said. Then they believed the Scripture and the words that Jesus had spoken.

Acts 3:15 — "You killed the author of life, but God raised him from the dead. We are witnesses of this."

Acts 4:33 — With great power the apostles continued to testify to the resurrection of

	the Lord Jesus, and much grace was with them all.
Romans 1:4	... and who through the Spirit of holiness was declared with power to be the Son of God by his resurrection from the dead: Jesus Christ our Lord.
1 Corinthians 15:3-8	For what I received I passed on to you as of first importance: that Christ died for our sins according to the Scriptures, ⁴that he was buried, that he was raised on the third day according to the Scriptures, ⁵and that he appeared to Peter, and then to the Twelve. ⁶After that, he appeared to more than five hundred of the brothers at the same time, most of whom are still living, though some have fallen asleep. ⁷Then he appeared to James, then to all the apostles, ⁸and last of all he appeared to me also, as to one abnormally born.
1 Corinthians 15:17	And if Christ has not been raised, your faith is futile; you are still in your sins.
Acts 1:9-11	After he said this, he was taken up before their very eyes, and a cloud hid him from their sight. ¹⁰They were looking intently up into the sky as he was going, when suddenly two men dressed in white stood beside them. ¹¹"Men of Galilee," they said, "why do you stand here looking into the sky? This same Jesus, who has been taken from you into heaven, will come back in the same way you have seen him go into heaven."
John 14:1-2	"Do not let your hearts be troubled. Trust in God; trust also in me. ²In my

	Father's house are many rooms; if it were not so, I would have told you. I am going there to prepare a place for you."
John 14:3	"And if I go and prepare a place for you, I will come back and take you to be with me that you also may be where I am."
Ephesians 1:18-23	I pray also that the eyes of your heart may be enlightened in order that you may know the hope to which he has called you, the riches of his glorious inheritance in the saints, [19]and his incomparably great power for us who believe. That power is like the working of his mighty strength, [20]which he exerted in Christ when he raised him from the dead and seated him at the right hand in the heavenly realms, [21]far above all rule and authority, power and dominion, and every title that can be given, not only in the present age but also in the one to come. [22]And God placed all things under his feet and appointed him to be head over everything for the church, [23]which is his body, the fullness of him who fills everything in every way.

Chapter Three: Eternal Life in Christ

John 3:36	"Whoever believes in the Son has eternal life, but whoever rejects the Son will not see life, for God's wrath remains on him."
John 14:6	Jesus answered, "I am the way and the truth and the life. No one comes to the Father except through me."
John 17:3	"Now this is eternal life: that they may know you, the only true God, and Jesus Christ, whom you have sent."
Acts 4:10-12	"Then know this, you and everyone else in Israel: It is by the name of Jesus Christ of Nazareth, whom you crucified but whom God raised from the dead, that this man stands before you completely healed. [11]He is 'the stone you builders rejected, which has become the capstone.' [12]Salvation is found in no one else, for there is no other name under heaven given to men by which we must be saved."
Romans 3:23	For all have sinned and fall short of the glory of God.

Romans 6:23	For the wages of sin is death, but the gift of God is eternal life in Christ Jesus our Lord.
John 1:12	Yet to all who received him, to those who believed in his name, he gave the right to become children of God.
John 11:25	Jesus said to her, "I am the resurrection and the life. He who believes in me will live, even though he dies."
Acts 10:43	"All the prophets testify about him that everyone who believes in him receives forgiveness of sins through his name."
1 John 5:11-12	And this is the testimony: God has given us eternal life, and this life is in his Son. [12]He who has the Son has life; he who does not have the Son of God does not have life.
Ephesians 2:8-9	For it is by grace you have been saved, through faith—and this not from yourselves, it is the gift of God—[9]not by works, so that no one can boast.
John 5:24	"I tell you the truth, whoever hears my word and believes him who sent me has eternal life and will not be condemned; he has crossed over from death to life."
Romans 8:35-39	Who shall separate us from the love of Christ? Shall trouble or hardship or persecution or famine or nakedness or danger or sword? [36]As it is written, "For your sake we face death all day long; we are considered as sheep to be slaughtered." [37]No, in all these things we are more than conquerors through him who loved us. [38]For I am convinced that neither death

	nor life, neither angels nor demons, neither the present nor the future, nor any powers, ³⁹neither height nor depth, nor anything else in all creation, will be able to separate us from the love of God that is in Christ Jesus our Lord.
2 Thessalonians 3:3	But the Lord is faithful, and he will strengthen and protect you from the evil one.
1 John 5:13	I write these things to you who believe in the name of the Son of God so that you may know that you have eternal life.
John 3:16	"For God so loved the world that he gave his one and only Son, that whoever believes in him shall not perish but have eternal life."

LifeChange

A NAVPRESS BIBLE STUDY SERIES

LifeChange Bible studies train you in good Bible study practices even as you enjoy a robust and engaging Bible study experience. Learn the skill as you study the Word. There is a study for every book of the Bible and relevant topics.

SINGLE COPIES AND BULK DISCOUNTS AT NAVPRESS.COM

CP1212